TRUCHAS

Closer to Heaven

TRUCHAS

Closer to Heaven

Chantal Guillemin

2015
Sugartown Publishing
Crockett, California

ISBN: 978-0-9913870-9-0

Sugartown Publishing
1164 Solano Ave., #140
Albany, CA 94706
www.sugartownpublishing.com

Cover art: weaving by Harry Córdova; photograph by Lobsang Wangdu
Frontispiece photo of author taken by Dan Bortko
Author photo: Lobsang Wangdu
Section photos: Chantal Guillemin and Dana Hart-Stone
Book design by Margaret Copeland, *terragrafix.com*

Printed in USA
by Minuteman Press
1101 Fifth Street
Berkeley, CA 94710
www.e-minutemanpress.com

Table of Contents

Llano Abeyta

La Naturaleza

Summertime

The High Road

Dedication

This book of poems is dedicated to my parents, Roger and Lucienne Guillemin, whose adventurous spirit led them to Truchas. They could not—and did not—escape the unique beauty of that part of the country. I thank them for imparting to me their deep appreciation of the landscape, the people, the history.

Foreword

In 1954, the road from the Rio Grande valley to Truchas had just been paved. My wife, Lucienne, and I took Road 76 for the first time, and though we lived in Houston and were visiting the Santa Fé area while attending a scientific conference, we knew we would be back. Sure enough, every year since, the whole family traveled to Truchas and stayed the summer. At first, we rented a room, then a house in town. The family became part of the community so much so that in 1964, villagers made an exception to the rule of not selling land to outsiders. We bought a beautiful twenty-acre parcel in *Llano Abeyta*, the westernmost hamlet of Truchas. Log by log, we dismantled a big hay barn and added it to an old two-room house. We manage to find an all-too-brief time each year to relax together in our family vacation home.

— *Roger Guillemin*

TRUCHAS

Closer to Heaven

On your travels through the Southwest, you may have driven through Truchas, New Mexico. For you, now, the village is more than a dot on the map and perhaps you wish to know more about the place. Beneath immense skies and the amphitheater of the Truchas peaks, behind adobe walls and the curtained windows of the village houses, stories are waiting to be told... waiting to be heard.

Last Weaver

Harry Córdova
inhales, exhales
with his loom.

Ochre, then sky blue
shuttle back
and forth,
back again.

Loosened skeins—
straw and marigold yarns
fill corner cubbyholes.

The opening door wakes
a tinkling brass bell.
Harry rests his legs,
makes small talk.

Visitors unroll
the finished rugs—all sizes—
on a pine-board floor.

When they leave,
Harry resumes
his dialogue
with the loom.

The Armoire

It needed new life.
Caked in dirt and stuffed
with boxes of pottery shards,
the dilapidated armoire sat
forgotten in the garage.

I vacuumed it top to bottom,
found and fashioned missing pieces,
discovered "Lupe Velez,"
handwritten in blue on one interior slat.

Was Lupe Velez, the same
María Guadalupe Velez,
spirited Mexican movie actress
who dated Clark Gable and Gary Cooper?

Did her sequined costumes, black lace,
and embroidered mantillas fill
this armoire with exotic fragrances?

Had her satin heels
and hatboxes full of fan mail
lined its floorboards?

Not until my Vegas sister, Kiki,
flew in with suitcases of cabaret props—
was that armoire
back in business.

Village Life

Remains of Their Home

Long gone—
the living room's woven curtains,
the cup-filled corner *trastero*,
the child's chair milled in her papa's shop,
the *nicho* where the Holy Virgin
visited to bless their home.

Left behind—
plate shards, a rusty apple corer,
a doll's plump leg.
Old bottle caps settle in the dust
where the workshop once stood.

Making her rounds in the village,
the Holy Virgin empties
her pockets of hope.

Vigas and *Latillas*

From the *Sangre de Cristo* forest
to the village below,
teams of burros pull carts
stacked with ax-felled pines.

At the homestead, hachets
chip away the bark,
smooth the trunks,
stroke the *vigas* and *latillas*
with flat, sharpened blades.

Hoisted atop adobe walls,
vigas span bedrooms, kitchens,
bear the weight of earthen rooves—
witness to generations.

Released by weathered walls,
vigas and *latillas* fall
pell-mell into the emptiness.

From car windows,
vacationers snap pictures
of the caved-in ceiling.

Stove Wood

The sawed wood
is axed
into stove-sized chunks.

For now, mounds
grow into piles
outside every house.

Inside, wood
feeds the furnace.
The kitchen warms.

Men on lunch break
come in,
hang up their coats.

Village Dog

No one cares that
a mangy mongrel
lost his battle with
a porcupine.

Canyon Dump

When men from Truchas
no longer made *tewas*,
they gave up hard-earned cash
to buy shoes and boots
at valley outfitters.

They brought home costly cans
of pitted and pre-sweetened fruit,
when women ceased putting by
backyard plums and chokecherry.

In the kitchen,
linoleum in long rolls hid
earthen floors cured with ox blood.
Vinyl-covered dinettes replaced
the wooden tables and chairs
tooled by fathers and uncles.

Corrugated roof toles
on houses, barns and pig sheds
were pulled off for shingles, asphalt.

They drove to the edge.
At the bottom:
the remains of Truchas
after the World War.

Ghost Pickup

Depressed pedals and gears
engage, pop, grind.
Wheels, columns, shafts
rotate, pivot, turn,
jive in synchrony
with the engine
disassembled and rebuilt
to last a lifetime.

Today, the wooden clatter
of the flatbed
used to haul hogs or
bales of alfalfa,
is all that still
drives my memory.

Oblivion

No one is ever there
to witness when
the old trucks
are pushed
over
the canyon's edge.

Mercantile

Mr. Fernandez sells milk, butter,
on occasion a few gallons of gas.
Mrs. Fernandez pencils my purchases
in an invoice pad, additions to our account.
A screen door snaps at my heels.

On the Taos road, the Martinez store is next
to the shortcut that runs along the ditch.
Floorboards creak as I browse hardware,
light streams illuminate bins of nails.

The post office is in Tafoya's General Store.
Mrs. Tafoya works the old-fashioned
cash register, and sorts mail,
while Reuben's mother looks on.
Sacks of beans, flour, lard, chainsaws, shoelaces,
cans of mink oil and chewing tobacco sit
side by side on tidy shelves.
Shovels, rakes and axes line the back wall.

My sisters and I stand in front of the counter
        candy jars,
point to jawbreakers, sourballs,
bubblegum, redhots and licorice sticks.
A hot day, we go for orange torpedoes
and pineapple popsickles.

The choice of postcards
disappoints the tourists.

La Gente

Descanso

Reform school to prison,
life started rough for Junior.
Shifting gears in his rebuilt pickup,
he skidded head on across an icy bridge,
into a truck loaded with freight.

He wears a suit in a coffin
lined with mauve pleated satin.
He leaves behind
a baby
and teenage Sofía.

The cross by the road
marks where he lost his life.
When you drive by, slow down,
stop,
pray for him.

La Celestina

Beside a plaster one-eared burro,
the Virgin and St. Francis greet visitors.

Tía Petra opens her door, invites you in.
You get a whiff of *canela*
coming from her woodburning stove.
She offers you a platter of *bizcochitos*.

As you talk of village news,
she parts her kitchen curtains to see
whose car ambles down the road.

Tía works as a lunchtime cook
for the *viejitos* at the Senior Center.

A plaque in her kitchen reads
"Familiarity breeds families":
Tía's matchmaking
does not always result
in marriage.

General Delivery

At first, it came on horseback
from Santa Cruz
to Ojo Sarco.

Afterwards,
in a two-wheeled sulky,
then by buggy,
then in a pickup.

In those days,
the mail came
Tuesday, Thursday, Saturday.

Then, there was
the parcel-post business,
the money-order business,
and savings bonds.

The boxes we use today,
I bought them myself.

My name is Manuel Martinez, Senior.
I was postmaster of Truchas
for forty-three years.

La Casa Azul

Brothers Henry, Kevin, and Michael,
all died young of liver disease, untreated cancer.
> *We fished and camped in Truchas Lake,*
> *rode horses in the mountains.*

Gloria married into heroin.
> *We laughed, cooked papas and tortillas*
> *in the blue house.*

Torturers left her son's decapitated body
in the Rio Grande.
Older sister, Josie, married at seventeen.
> *On our way to the fountain, we flirted*
> *with low-riders cruising main street.*

Her sons leave as soon as they can.
Eva, grandmother at thirty,
grieves into death
for her too-early departed.
> *We roasted chile verde in her oven,*
> *helped her make beds, hang up the wash.*

Henry Senior, goes on living
alone in the blue house.

The Visit

At fourteen,
I knitted Nelsito a sweater
with blended wool,
black and yellow,
wrote him torrid love letters.

We rode double
bareback on a paint,
in the mountain forest,
his curly black hair—
stiff with gel.

At eighteen, he fell in with June,
and had May, a baby girl.

Fifty years seem to melt away
when I visit my teenage love
in the *camposanto*.

Until He Died

Before, there weren't any doctors.
People kept a watch over the person
until he died,
giving him remedies—
the Mexican medicinal herbs
people used in those days.
People didn't know
what was wrong with them.
They got sick,
had fever,
temperature,
and died.
There was no way
to save people.
Now, if one gets sick,
everybody comes to see him,
to watch over him.

— Spoken by Canuto Martinez

Big Night Out

It was dangerous for Anglos
in the old part of Truchas.
I knew this but let myself be bullied
into going to the pool hall that night.
Marsha, the minister's daughter,
my sisters and I climbed
into the station wagon.

As we walked through double doors,
I saw Isabro, the village bad seed.
We made an about-face and ran.
I fumbled with the keys. We rushed in.
Up front sat Isabro, his switchblade
pressed against Kiki's throat.
The motor running,
my foot was on the brake.

Marsha's calm voice rising from the back
mimicked her father's ministerial manner.
She asked Isabro about his family, his life.
A whole hour passed.
Mollified, he lowered the blade
and rolled out of the car.
As we drove away, he shouted,
promised to burn our house down.
We packed Warpaint, the other horses,
spent the next week camping
in the mountain safehold.

Jerri's Last Spring

Jerri went on the lam
after he shot the village bully,
a known drug trafficker,
point-blank.

When the caretaker, Mr. Trujillo
opened our house, he found
Jerri's decomposing body
in the back bedroom,
a month after the manhunt
in Rio Arriba county
was called off.

After that,
service vehicles and heavy boots
trampled emerging grasses
around the house.
Noises of compressed gravel
and slamming car doors
alarmed nesting jays and magpies.
The delicate fragrance of
iris and lilac filled
the nostrils of intruders.

Art Scene *Trucheros*

buy houses, the Martinez store,
even the Pentacostal church,
remodel them into arts-and-crafts stores
to appeal to passersby, collectors.
Weekend visitors desperate for souvenirs,
carry home art, a rag rug, a book of poems.
Gallery owners and artists make a good living
from their sales of paintings and sculpture.
Adult children seldom visit, wonder why
their parents would want to live
in a place so rustic and remote.
They dread the day they will
have to bury them.

Acequia

When the mayordomo says
to go clean the acequia de la sierra,
we have to go clean it.
To every four acres,
you have to put one man to work.
I got twenty-one acres,
so I have to put five men
on the ditch every day.
The mayordomo gives the water to the people.
The water belongs to him.

When I irrigate,
I have so many hours per acre.
If you got one acre, he give you
two hours, two and a half hours,
and that's all he give.
If you got twenty, thirty acres,
he give so many more hours.
And he watches the water
to see I don't irrigate down below or
cut water over here.
He comes over here
and prosecutes me.

— Spoken by Apolinar Sandoval

Water Hoarder

This man is a frog:
he always has water.
He fights a lot with the people of the llano
for the water, they tell me.
He cuts off the water, sometimes.
People have to complain to the mayordomo.
He's very covetous of water,
that's why he is a frog.

— Spoken by Canuto Martinez

Llano Abeyta

La Morada de Llano Abeyta

Rainwater wore away
the walls of the old *morada*.
No gloves patted new skin.

No tools fitted a new door
to the deserted chapel.
Swallow nests hang
from the beam ceiling.

No new bell was cast
to replace the one missing
from the plank steeple.

Only silence calls the faithful.

Dry Storm

Curtains billow, a door slams.
Hollyhock leaves shiver.
The rhubarb's papery seeds scatter
as winds sweep over *Llano Abeyta*.
In the canyons, thunder rumbles,
a hawk soars on updrafts.
Ripples in the pond reflect gray,
surly clouds.

No rush to check car windows,
bring in sheets from the line.

Dry Summer

No one hears
the chatter of tumbling water.

The ditch runs dry
in *Llano Abeyta,*
Truchas' lowest hamlet.

Locks stay open.
Vegetation along the banks
is sparse.

Ponds are empty.

In the village, some recall
how no snow fell
on the peaks last winter.

Some say that,
when no one is watching,
water gets diverted
from the *acequia madre.*

Sobrante

The water is very inconstant in Llano Abeyta.
If the water isn't used over here,
it goes down the ditch down there—
that's when you have water in Llano Abeyta.
Llano Abeyta gets the sobrante.
People here don't want to admit it—
it has the right only when there is lots of water.
If the water is used up here,
no water for Llano Abeyta.
That's the way it goes.
Like this year, we get the water when we want it.
We've been making pretty good.

— Spoken by Apolinar and Donicio Sandoval

Ditch

Ditch willows thicken.
Sticks, leaves, old trash
slow the rush of water.
Fields soak up the overflow.

Village ditch cleaners are idle.
Their leader—the one who trains race horses
is on a winning streak.

To Cut Willow

Stand in the stream to reach the willow;
   His hand touched my elbow.
Sever the base of young, leafy stems;
   Waves of pleasure washed over me.
Stack willow branches next to the road;
   He said he didn't live here anymore, that he was visiting
   his mother. That I should drop in and visit her, if I could.
Transfer the pile to the wheelbarrow;
   I saw myself in his black eyes, I said I would.
Empty the load close to the stack of kindling
for use next year;
   He climbed in his truck and sped away.
If you ever cut willow again,
don't do it alone.

Roadside Collection

There's no telling what you'll find
when you pick up trash in *el llano*:
a tight bundle next to a cow patty
turns out to be a soiled diaper;
a plastic bag trapped in the willows
luffs in the wind like a jib.
Yards from the road,
constellations of cans
glint in the noonday sun.

When you pick up a beer bottle
tossed out of a car,
look for the stinkbug
sheltering inside.

Before you throw away red plastic roses,
check to see, if they fell off the *descanso*
erected by the grieving family
of Epiphanio Trujillo.

When you are surprised by the dead coyote—
his tail still fluffy—
hanging upside down from the fencepost,
run home,
faster
than the bullet that got him.

Fencelines

Coiled in a tangled trap,
rusty barbed-wire,
replaced by taut, new steel,
waits for unwary hooves,
the tender pads
of coyotes.

While We Sleep

the roots of the cottonwood
drain the pond;

frogs burrow deep, below the frost line,
turn mealy white;

coyotes corner stiff-legged dogs,
cut out calves from the herd;

an *acequia* lock is lifted,
precious water goes unaccounted.

A childhood friend—
addicted to heroin—
can't feed his family
in *el llano*.

Dirt Road

After a hard rain,
intrepid tires redraw its edges.
Slippery mud usurps steering,
sends heavy trucks sideways,
into the ditch.
Boards top the stubbornest grooves;
loose cattle press their hooves
into stenciled patterns left by tires.
Sky and clouds linger in puddles,
mirroring double rainbows
and faces of foot-travelers
dragging their adobe mud boots
to the post-office
or Tafoya's General Store.

When the road dries out,
the mica-flecked clay
crumbles like flour.

Afternoon Walk

I walk along the gravel road,
past the ancient ant hill,
and the rose-hip thicket,
toward the juniper.

A faraway truck gears down
the valley road.

The neighbor's dog crosses the field,
his fur hides scabs, old scars.

Willow stands crowd the ditch bed,
slow the downhill flow
to Padilla's pond.

Three tail-swishing horses
stand in the heat
at the gate.

Tomorrow,
I'll loosen the heavy chain
that holds it to the post,
and slip out.

La Naturaleza

If You Stay Long Enough

you may see the black cat
slink through the sagebrush,
dash toward the *piñon*;

you may feel the brunt of winter
on the windblown *llano*;

you may hear the silence
as clouds form and evaporate
over the granite mountain.

Picture Window

Beyond parted curtains
stand seed-studded
mullein spires.

Fluttering petals of
pink and white cosmos
call to flies and bees: one last sip
of pollen and nectar.

In that shallow pond,
Samuelita drowned.
Now, I watch the long-legged heron spear
frogs and salamanders.

Under snow-filled clouds,
the *Sangre de Cristo*
wears a patchwork of russet and gold.

Pond Life

Under the hot summer sun,
walk-on-water spiders
follow their mud shadows.

Snakes swim sideways,
herd tadpoles for lunch.

From their silt sheets,
sleepy salamanders
come up for air.

I sit under the parasol,
watch coupled damselflies
dart
    hover
        then dart again.

I Forget Why

the cottonwood should not be allowed
to grow a forest of its own kind.
Year after year,
it sends new shoots
into the summer sky.
And every year,
I remove them from the hillside.

Patch

After the fire,
rangers in sage-green trucks
replant the wasteland.

Equidistant saplings
grow in unison.

After fifty years,
you still couldn't
call this a forest.

Stump Sprout

Charged to sustain
the roots of the giant,
lassoed, felled and quartered
by the roaring blade,
a flurry of leaves
on the side of the stump
quivers in the clearing.

My Family's Tree

Under the canopy
of the old peach tree,
the wind is quiet,
bees hum.

Pale burdock leaves
grow undisturbed
beneath the trunk,
which over the years,
has grown massive,
horizontal.

Resin exudes
from the black bark,
traps
a down feather.

White Peaches

If the fruit matures at all,
it will be when the
first snows of late October
blanket the *Sangre de Cristo*.

Revenge of the Cockleburs

They menace our city clothes
in their rusty ripeness,
ready to spring out with
spiny balls covered in seed hooks.

They taunt our fleece jackets
with barbed insults,
hurl out threats of revenge.

Cockleburs snag
our sacrificial sweaters,
as we wrestle the severed plants
into black cinch bags.

Next day, thousands of seeds
travel with us
to fertile new ground.

It's Time

for dandelion umbels
to make their wind-borne journey.

Some land near the ant hill.

Others descend and float on the pond.

Most drop in the field.

Falling Stars

We stand in
the night sky
because Truchas is
closer to heaven.

Small stars streak past:
exclamation marks
punctuating space
between constellations.

Startled by the sudden light
of the meteor shower,
the celestial muses cluster
behind a smoky veil.

The Perseids perform
backstage encores
when dawn's curtain
rises on the horizon.

Summertime

Dump Dog

Holding my breath,
I hurl bags of trash
into the ravine.

Below: a graveyard of broken furniture,
emptied lard buckets, smoldering debris.

A puppy scrambles over rusty cans.

The car idles.
Acrid smoke fills the air.

As the car heads home,
I hold her close.

The Rescue

After an all-night struggle to escape,
the kestrel floats in a horse trough.
Mother scoops up the raptor,
lays it on the picnic table.
She warms him
with her electric hair-dryer.
The kestrel stirs,
quivers,
flops around,
suddenly takes flight,
then vanishes
into the *piñon*.

Piñon Pie

Soak pitted prunes and apricots overnight.
Line pie crust with apricot jam.
Cut plump prunes and apricots into small pieces,
sprinkle them over the jam.
Mix softened butter with orange zest,
dab over fruit.
Add a layer of pine nuts.
Bake in a hot oven.

Serve in small portions
with a cup of hot tea
on an August afternoon,
after the storm has passed
and double rainbows
arch over the canyons.

Throw a new log on the fire.

New Fire

Mother gets up,
sweeps out
yesterday's ashes
from the fireplace.

Balled newspapers,
sticks, logs, a match
to build the new fire.

The room's cold edge
begins to thaw. Feet find
slippers under beds—
we shuffle to the crackling blaze.

Kindling

Fields and canyons yield obvious sticks.
Cedar is plentiful.

We need gloves for
tugging and twisting
dry sagebrush.

Willow cuttings, now too green—
ready next year.

If you rely on a fireplace
for warmth,
the search for kindling is unending.

It is as if

the sticks of firewood you shape with an ax
are too precious to burn;
the cosmos petals never froze
that October morning;
the fruit tree was never planted
and forgotten behind the lilac;
I never left you waving
in my rear-view mirror.

Summertime

Will anyone notice that
I didn't measure the coffee
before brewing it?

That the hook
to the back door
was not latched
last night?

That the wasp that wandered
past the screen door,
bumped all morning
against the closed windows?

That the gardening tools
next to the pile of dried iris
are still where I left them?

Waiting Garden

Posts, askew
in their holes,
mark the perimeter.
Barren gooseberry bushes
subsist in the corner.
Trapped tumbleweeds
collect over phantom rows.
Mounds of ashes,
dumped in haste
over the fence,
harden.

In this patch of field,
even the wind's weed seeds
won't grow.

Hollyhocks

Heart-shaped leaves, rough as sandpaper
push up to the ionosphere
while greedy roots pursue elusive aquifers.

They put out papery blooms,
singles and doubles in chalky white,
    morning-sky pink,
        cactus-fruit rose,
            chili-powder red.

The Vigil girls flip the frilly petals
to make doll dresses,
create ballerinas wearing tutus.

When hollyhocks grow between the flagstones,
Mother's frown banishes them
to the burn pile.

Brittle Bouquet

She stoops to pluck
brittle stems for
her earthen pot bouquet.

At summer's end, plant life
in all shades of dry,
stands rife with seeds.

The screen door opens.
Mother, at ninety-two
returns from the back field.

Typical Day

At the pond, she nets the scum,
points to camouflaged salamanders
basking in underwater sun heat.

I drive her to the post office—
her chance to talk with old friends,
pick up her letters from France.

Despite her recent mini-stroke,
she studies Chinese, reads history,
beats Father and me at Scrabble.

After the game show on French T.V.,
she starts dinner, serves what Father likes,
salmon or pork loin panfried in butter.

A host of pills waits for Mother.
She swallows the vitamins first,
then blood thinners.

Dishes can wait 'til tomorrow.

Breakfast

Wrapped in a kimono,
Father savors coffee
with a splash of milk.
Mother stirs in a sugar cube.

The world awakes
to their plans for the day:
reading newspapers,
readying for visitors.

I hear her warning
through the swinging door:
"You'll blow a fuse if you use
the toaster and the microwave
at the same time."

Father

His back to the mountain,
   he knows
      how many clouds have gathered
      beyond the peaks.

C.B.

We never knew when Father
would check up on us girls,
so we had to stay within range.

After making beds at Josie's and Gloria's,
we were dying to cruise main street,
hang out at the fountain.

We'd take off right after he'd call.
One minute, we'd be palm-flapping *tortillas*,
the next, we'd be riding up the mountains
in the back of an old pickup.

The C.B. was retired when
Josie got married.

Riding Double in a Hail Storm

As we rode Warpaint,
the pinto from *el llano*,
Nelsito and I did not notice
the ice clouds gather
in the summer sky.

An outburst of hail crashed over us.
Icy drops burned our skin.
We found cover deep in the forest,
rode out the storm pressed
against a tree trunk.

Warpaint stepped up the pace
on the way back to the village.
I wanted to freeze time.

History of Dirty Clothes

I rolled the turquoise pants
to clean out the ditch, sweep.
The black ones pushed
wheelbarrows full of firewood.
I had on the green ones
when I baked *piñon* pie,
went to town to visit friends.
I made butternut squash soup
and played Scrabble with Mother
wearing the blue and white shirt.
When I fixed the wine rack,
I wore the brown-striped sweater.

Today is laundry day.
Another chance to make history.

Pottery Puzzle

On a family field trip at Puyé cliffs,
we pick up and pocket
fragments of Pueblo pottery.

At the table, we arrange,
rearrange the shards,
in search of patterns,
matching edges.

Decades later, the painted
thin parallel black lines
are scrutinized again.

They let out no secrets.

My Truchas Bed

A hand-stitched quilt
of yesteryear's scraps—
children's aprons and shirts—
covers the bed.

A single bed for my old cat and me...

Flies buzz above at paint-spattered panes.
A book, opened flat, slips to the floor.

My dried mud feet hang off the edge,
to keep the sheets clean.

Summer Afternoon

From my bed,
I heard sprinkles,
not really rain:
soft paws
on the corrugated roof.

Then, silence.

The Dart

I can't see the scar
where the dart
you threw at me
punctured my back.

The steel point—
I pulled out.
Your message—
I haven't forgotten.

Break-In

Isabro forces the door,
ransacks the house.

In his loot bag,
everyday knives, forks and spoons
are a jumbled mass.

We post *kachinas* and *santos*
throughout our living room—
sentinels against crime.

If we had more faith,
perhaps they would keep better watch.

Closing Checklist

Before you close the house,
Ring the bell—one last time.
Close and lift out umbrella.
Roll in redwood picnic table.
Lower flags and fold.
Notice first snow on peaks.
Feel chill air of fall.
Take carrots to white horse in Padilla's field.
Stop water flow to pond.
Scrape shovel clean.
Drain and coil garden hoses.
Collect hollyhock and cosmos seed.
Stare out curtainless windows.
Pack *kachinas*—keep upright.
Shake kilims—roll up and stack.
Hear your footsteps echo in rooms.
Box thousand-piece puzzle.
Give yourself a silent pep talk.
Feel your heart tighten anyway.
Wrap San Rafael, patron saint
of travelers, in newsprint.
Use up perishables for last meal.
Drop in on friends with food giveaway box.
Load car.
Close and hook shutters from the inside.
Shut gate, close padlock over chain.
Try not to look back
as car descends
to the valley.

The High Road

Bypass

At the highest, most centrifugal point
of the hairpin curve,
passengers traveling from Truchas to Santa Cruz
got a panoramic view of
Truchas Peaks, the Rio Grande valley,
the Jemez range and Pedernal.
Lives were lost on that section
of old Road 76.
The hill was surveyed,
the road straightened
to conform to the new grade.
Dead man's curve was bypassed.

After drinking with his *primos*,
Arturo, still in his teenage years,
drives off the road and dies
on new Road 76.

June Frost

Apple trees in Chimayó
bear no fruit.

No plums, peaches, apricots
for sale at empty roadside stands.

In Dixon and Velarde,
grape growers harvest no clusters
to press and ferment.

Unless winemakers buy grapes
from other regions, there will be
no new wine bottled next year.

History in a Phonebook

Just open the Española one
and look under Cundiyó.
You'll see that all the listings
have the same last name.

It all started with José Antonio Vigil,
defender against Comanche raids.
Chief Capitán Corona,
whose partially scalped hair
regrew in a crown-like bunch,
coveted Vigil's horse, *El Alazán.*
He ambushed Vigil to steal the horse
but was killed by Vigil instead.

Local hero Vigil was renamed el Capitán Vigil.
He and his eight sons founded Cundiyó
and today, their descendants—
all named Vigil—
reside in Cundiyó.

Vallero Star

To escape Comanche raids and disease,
a few families left Las Trampas.
In the heart of the forest,
they established El Valle.

Local earth, flecked with mica, daubs
the interior walls of the church's apse:
tiny points of starlight to inspire
weaver Patricia Montoya.

Her legs lacked strength
to press down on the treadles,
so her parents designed and built
a hand-operated loom for her.

Patricia wove stars into her work.

Her diamond-shaped pattern
in eight points of contrasting colors,
is still in use by weavers today.

San José de Gracia

If the old church door is locked,
walk down the weedy path
toward the barking dog.
He belongs to Mr. O.,
the keeper of the key
to the church in Las Trampas.

Beyond the carved ceiling and portals,
in the penumbra of the cool, quiet church,
reredos, lifesize painted panels
depicting the most popular saints,
lean against the walls.

Well-worn floor boards lead up
to the altar lit by filtered sun.

On chilly days, a wood stove warms
the congregation.

Women of the village recently applied
a waterproof coating of straw-filled mud
to the thick outer adobe.

When summers are dry and food
is scarce, bears come down
from the forested hills to eat
Mr. O.'s plums.

Peñasco

A portable carnival unfolds
on the rocky terrain.
Villagers from nearby towns
ride the ferris-wheel, sip pop,
relish mustard-covered hotdogs,
mouth at cotton candy.
Parading down the street,
men on horseback wear metal helmets,
carry lances to re-enact the victory
of the Spanish over the Pueblos.
In her white, lacy dress,
this year's fiesta queen,
rides on the hood of a convertible
dotted with tissue carnations.
Parked vehicles are filled
with friends and relatives
catching up on local news.

Old news was that Dr. Horace Taylor,
Anglo, set up his medical practice
in *Peñasco*, where he once attended
the pregnant wife of a jealous husband.

Though he saved her life, he was ambushed,
nearly killed by a group of angry men.
He promptly closed his practice.

Lately, mock accidents are staged
along the roadsides.
Tourists stop, are held up at gunpoint.

Times are tough in *Peñasco*.

Ku Sehn Pin (Stone Man Mountain)

The cumulous crown,
the setting sun's light on its rock flank,
the leaves of its aspen forest,
the summer scent of turpentine,
its hurrying streams,
strawberries, wild and sweet,
its chorus of grasshoppers,
its glacial lake, sacred to the Tewa,
the home I take home.

Reading Poems in the Car

Ask your passenger to read the poems.
If you are between Truchas and Ojo Sarco,
you see roadside flowers,
pines infested with black beetle borers,
hawks flying above, woodcutters' trails.
Loose horses or cattle scrounge for
young grass on the shoulders.

Ask your passenger to turn the pages.
You may be stuck behind a pickup
hauling a cord of firewood.
If you plan to stop at
Mission *San José de Gracia*
in Las Trampas,
visit the shopkeeper across the lot:
He's a storyteller and
has cold sodas in the fridge.
On your right, past the church,
there's a *canoa*, an elevated water canal
carved out of a tree that spans the canyon.

Ask your passenger to earmark pages
of poems you want to reread.
If you are on the meandering road
between Chamisal and Vadito,
you may be distracted by the fall colors.
Chamisa, used as a natural maize-colored dye
by weavers years ago,
grows along both sides of the road.

It takes two to read poems in the car.

A Brief History of Truchas

The village of Truchas is located at the base of the amphitheater of the *Sangre de Cristo* mountains in the southern Rockies of northern New Mexico. At 8,400 feet in altitude, it is perched on the edge of a precipice that overlooks the Jemez Range and the Rio Grande Valley.

The people of Tewa ancestry inhabited the Truchas area 200 years before the arrival of the Spanish in the early 16th century. These Pueblo people began a network of hand-dug ditches from the base of the peaks to bring water for crop irrigation and domestic use. They excavated micaceous clay for pottery making and conducted a lively trade with other Pueblo communities in the Rio Grande Valley. Settlement remains include stone foundations, pottery shards and human bones, which sometimes get mixed into the mud stucco applied to protect the outer adobe walls of houses.

Pueblo Tewa speakers consider South Truchas Peak their sacred mountain of the East, *Ku Sehn Pin* (Stone Man Mountain) and refer to the Truchas river basin as their eastern homeland. Revered entities watch over the Tewa world from the top of the mountain and up until the early 1900s, the people of Ohkay Owingeh, formerly known as San Juan Pueblo, made religious pilgrimages to Truchas Peak.

Truchas was founded in 1754 as a Spanish outpost to guard the region against raiding Comanches and Kiowa Indians and as an incentive for Hispanic colonization. For protection, the village of Truchas was built within fortress walls around two interior plazas dominated by round stone and adobe watch towers. Though still visible in the middle of the 20th century, these *torreónes* have since crumbled.

During the 18th century, Comanche and Jicarilla Apache often attacked Truchas' northern and eastern borders. Eventually, Pueblo and Hispanic villages formed alliances to repel these nomadic invaders. Comanche raids ended in 1786 with the signing of a formal treaty.

Under the able governorship of Tomás Velez Cachupín, settlers from Chimayó and Córdova petitioned for a land grant to provide them with material resources such as pastureland, water and timber. As a representative of the Spanish Crown (Mexico gained its independence from Spain in 1821), Cachupín granted them shares of forest land in the 14,786 acre *Nuestra Señora del Rosario, San Fernando y Santiago del Río de las Truchas* grant. Since then, grant shareholders have relied on the region's bounty. The settlers and their descendants managed, maintained and extended the network of existing ditches. In recent times, dynamite was used to blast huge boulders which had rolled downstream, carried along by raging torrents of melted snows.

Families maintained vegetable gardens and grew beans, peas, corn, oats, wheat, potatoes and squash. This subsistence agriculture was supplemented by hunting buffalo and deer, and fishing. Villagers cultivated alfalfa to provide fodder for animals during the rigorous winter months. They herded sheep and goats, raised pigs and relied on donkeys to transport firewood. At one time, over 6,500 goats grazed in the forested area above Truchas. National forest permits became prohibitively costly so cattle were raised instead; they could be sold at a higher price than the goats. The goats threshed the wheat with their sharp hooves until 1918 when a threshing machine was purchased. The wheat was ground into flour by eight mills installed on the ditch. Villagers then bartered the flour for salt, sugar, rice and coffee which they bought in the village's grocery stores. Growers from neighboring valley villages sold fresh *chile* and apples from their pickup trucks to the residents of Truchas.

To pay for goods, several generations of *Trucheros* have had to work outside the village. Men worked on the railroad in Colorado, tended sheep in Wyoming, and mined uranium in the western New Mexico town of Grants. Once the road from the valley was paved, they commuted to jobs at the National Laboratories in Los Alamos and to Santa Fé. Many families benefited from employment in Los Alamos as they were able to afford modern time-saving appliances and pay for home improvements.

During the Depression, Truchas produced poles and beams to build a movie theater in San Ildefonso, one of six Tewa pueblos located in the Rio Grande Valley. A sawmill was set up in the forest and logging continued for decades.

In their relative isolation, *Trucheros* were self-sufficient. They formed organizations, both religious and secular for mutual protection, well-being, and the fair distribution of resources. Project-oriented groups of villagers dug and maintained a community well which facilitated water conveyance to homes, established fire departments, and built a clinic. The clinic, originally staffed by visiting doctors and nurses, was spearheaded by Presbytarian missionaries who — since the 1880s —travelled to remote villages like Truchas to bring medical relief to the people. Dr. Anthony Sandoval, who set up his practice in Los Alamos, is a noted cardiologist from Truchas.

Early settlers brought with them religious traditions including the roots of *Penitente* beliefs. *Penitentes* seek to emulate Christ's life and suffering. During *Semana Santa*, Holy Week, they pray, sing mournful *alabados* and reenact the Passion of Christ. The rest of the year when they are not fulfilling religious duties, they assist families in need. When someone dies, they bring food, make the coffin, help conduct the wake, dig the grave, take care of chores such as harvest crops, chop wood, care for stock, and nurse the sick. In the past, they commissioned *santeros* to carve and paint religious figures and panels which they kept in the *moradas* or used in processions. *Santero* Pedro Antonio Fresquís (1749-1831), also called the Truchas Master, is well known for his Holy Trinity and Our Lady of Mount Carmel in the collection of the Brooklyn Museum.

In the 1960s and 70s, young people from outside the region who sought simpler lifestyles began moving to Truchas. Though many non-Hispanics live in Truchas today, there was a time when visitors were met with hostility. Land sales or exchanges only took place between family members.

The introduction of drugs to the village is the cause of grief, violence, and deaths in many families.

Today, Truchas has a lively art scene with over fifteen galleries and artist studios that sell art in a wide range of media and styles. The number of artists and galleries participating in the income-generating High Road Art Tour has increased steadily since its inception, fifteen years ago. The tour takes place during the two last weekends in September. The art community is closely linked and extends to artists in other villages along the High Road. Facilities such as bed and breakfasts and a conference center make it easy for visitors to spend time in Truchas.

Truchas is a village in transition and is currently home to about 560 people.

— *Chantal Guillemin, 2014*

Glossary

Acequia — derived from the Arabic *saqa*, to irrigate; an irrigation ditch.

Acequia madre — mother ditch or main ditch which brings water from the mountains to the village and surrounding fields.

Alabados — sorrowful hymns sung by the *Penitentes* to praise or glorify the Passion of Christ.

Azul — blue.

Bizcochito — rich cookie speckled with anise seed, dusted with sugar and cinnamon.

Camposanto — cemetery, graveyard.

Canela — cinnamon.

Canoa — hand-hewn log flume used to channel water across ravines.

Casa — house.

Celestina — lover's go-between, a matchmaker.

Chile — red or green chili pepper (*verde*).

Descanso — a roadside shrine marked with a cross to indicate where death overtook a loved one, usually in an automobile accident. In the past, pall bearers rested there while carrying a coffin for burial. Prayers for the dead are requested when passersby come upon such a cross.

Gente — people.

Kachina — carved and painted wooden figures used as teaching aids in Pueblo religions. *Kachinas* bring to life the spirit world of the Hopi and Zuñi Indians.

Ku Sehn Pin — Tewa name for South Truchas Peak; translates as Stone Man Mountain.

Latíllas — peeled saplings placed on ceiling beams either at right angles or in a herringbone pattern.

Llano — area of flat ground.

Llano Abeyta — westernmost hamlet of Truchas.

Mayordomo — water manager whose duties are to oversee spring cleaning and repair of the irrigation canals, ensure equitable distribution of water, resolve disputes, and watch for water thieves.

Morada — roadside chapel built with massive walls and no windows; used by the *Penitentes* during Holy Week as a chapter meeting house and chapel.

Naturaleza — nature.

Nicho — functional recess in interior walls used to highlight prized possessions.

Papas — potatoes, peeled, sliced and sautéed in lard.

Peñasco — big rock; town on the High Road with a population of 589, estimated per capita income is $15,742.

Penitentes — also called *Los Hermanos Penitentes* — the Penitente Brotherhood; grassroot movement, independent of the Church; religious association of men who found solace in sharing the suffering of Christ whom they worshipped and emulated.

Piñon — piñon pine produce nuts in quantity only every six years at a given location. Tiny, edible nuts contain over 3,000 calories per pound and are a valuable food. Nuts are sometimes collected during family outings.

Primo — male cousin, a buddy.

Reredos — lifesize panels of popular saints positioned in a church against the walls of the apse.

Sangre de Cristo — means blood of Christ and is the name given to the northern New Mexico mountain range in which Truchas is located. It may have been called thus because of the activities of the *Penitentes* during Holy Week which have included flagellation and crucifixion in memory of the Passion of Christ.

Santo — a saint; wooden religious figures often carved out of cottonwood or pine; often commissioned by the

Penitentes for the *moradas* or for processions during Holy Week.

Santeros — itinerant wood carvers, who carved and coated wooden religious figures or panels with gesso and painted them with vegetable dyes and pulverized clays.

Semana Santa — Holy Week, the week before Easter.

Sierra — mountains.

Sobrante — remainder, surplus.

Tewa — a Pueblo people and language.

Tewas — mocassins made of rawhide.

Torreónes — towers used as lookouts.

Tortillas — flat bread made of wheat flour and cooked on a griddle or skillet.

Trampas — the traps; founded in 1751 by Juan de Arguello.

Trastero — large, upright, free-standing kitchen cupboard often used for storing dishes.

Truchas — named for the Rio Truchas ("trout river").

Truchero — inhabitant of Truchas.

Vallero — from El Valle, which means valley; weaving design identified by use of an eight-pointed star.

Viejitos — old people.

Vigas — a wood ceiling beam made of pine or fir, pealed of its bark and twigs.

Acknowledgments

Alvaro and Barbara Cardona-Hine, Judith Hert, Jannie Dresser, Barbara Minton, Rita Flores Bogaert, David White, Ellen Levin, Kimberly Satterfield, Jessica Levine, Madeline Lacques-Aranda, Robin Michel, Saddika, Elizabeth Claman, Adam David Miller, Jane Armbruster, Marcia Rein, Mickey Ellinger, Jon Gilgoff, Penelope La Montagne, Patricia Nelson, and Lila Wahrhaftig offered insights and guided my editing efforts as I wrote and assembled the collection of poems in *Truchas: Closer to Heaven*. For this I am ever so grateful.

About the Author

Chantal Guillemin traces her roots to France, from where her parents emigrated in 1948. Her childhood was spent in Texas, New Mexico and France. She studied printmaking and the history of photography at the University of New Mexico where she also spent a year as curator-fellow at Tamarind Institute. In the early 1970's, she spent a summer interviewing the oldest residents of Truchas under the guidance of anthropologist Edward T. Hall. She worked for Larry Bell as studio assistant when he first developed his vapor drawings on paper. In California, she has held jobs in a variety of fields: art, property management, publishing, and higher education. As a self-appointed ambassador for Truchas, Chantal has talked about Truchas all her life. In her yearly pilgrimage to Truchas, she renews her relationship with northern New Mexico, with old friends, and with her muse.

She is married to Guy Birenbaum and lives in Richmond, California, when she is not able to be in Truchas. This is her first book.

Thee do I crave co-partner in that verse
Which I presume on Nature to compose...
Divine one, give my words
Immortal charm.
— *Lucretius, 50 BCE, De Rerum Natura*

Sugartown Publishing

Based in Crockett, California, home to the famous C&H Sugar plant.

Sugartown Publishing joined a long-established tradition of
cooperative publishing in 2012. We are dedicated to bringing
into print, electronic and audio media formats *works of
literary merit that have something significant to say.*

Current and forthcoming titles include:

A Stalwart Bends, Poems and Reflections, by Ben Slomoff (2012).
Doing Time With Nehru, memoir by Yin Marsh (2012).
Among the Shapes that Fold and Fly, poetry by Patricia Nelson (2013).
Between the Fault Lines: Eight East Bay Poets, edited by Jannie M. Dresser (2013).
Workers' Compensation: Poems of Labor & the Working Life, by Jannie M. Dresser (2013).
Swimming the Sky, poetry by Gail Peterson (2013).
It Lasts a Moment: New & Collected Poems, by Fred Ostrander (2013).
Falling Home, poetry by Gary Turchin (2013).
Voices from the Field, poetry by Kimberly Satterfield (2013).
At My Table, poetry by Judith Yamamoto (2013).
The Glass Ship, prose-poems by Judy Wells (2014).
Yew Nork, poetry by Dale Jensen (2014).
Truchas: Closer to Heaven, poetry by Chantal Guillemin (2015).

Contact us for more information on how we can help you get your book into print.

sugartownpublishing.com
janniedres@att.net
Mailing address:
1164 Solano Ave. #140,
Albany, CA 94706